The Thought Store

The Thought Store

8 Simple Thinking Habits for Work and Life

Jeanne Marian Nangle

www.8SimpleThinkingHabits.com

Published by Jeanne Nangle Consulting
El Dorado Hills, CA 95762

Cover illustration and interior illustrations: Alex Hartong
Interior layout: Kathryn Marcellino

Library of Congress Control Number: 2014917456

ISBN 978-0-9851635-2-5

To Jared and Jonah,

May your thoughts align
with what you are here to do,
and who you are meant to be.

Acknowledgments

I would like to extend my heartfelt gratitude to the following people who have helped and supported me during the formation of this book.

First, to my cover artist, Alex Hartong, whose patience and willingness to create the most incredible thoughts in print made this process a joy. You are a gifted artist and wonderful person. Thank you to Desiree Aragon Nielson for helping me be who and what I am capable of being. I am deeply grateful for you. Also, thank you for reminding me: "The story is about Henry!" Thanks to Mollie Nielson for your enthusiasm about thoughts. Debra Gussin, thank you very much for your insight, encouragement, and lifelong friendship. A special thank you to Dorothy Walker Wright for sharing your gifts and bringing me much needed clarity at precisely the right time.

My heartfelt gratitude to Carrie Grip, a soulmate for many years. Many thanks to Carol Eschelmann for helping me with my subtitle. Thank you Cam Conley for listening. Thank you Dave Bischoff for being there in ways small and large. Joan Laufenberg, thanks for saying you loved my first chapter when I needed to hear it. Dr. Leslie Reed, thank you for being the voice in my head. A big thank you to the Smyte family: Steve, Rose, Alex and Julia, for showing us that a good meal puts things in a brighter light. Thank you Drew and Lois Horning for all you do and who you are. Thank you Tom and Tina Farmer for your constant love and support. And Dannele, thank you for being my dear friend over the years and miles.

Thank you to Lani Dodd for editing my questionable grammar. Any remaining errors are my fault! Much thanks to Kathryn Marcellino, for designing the interior layout and sending this book off in its proper form.

My deepest thanks to the many great thinkers in print who've made me a better thinker.

A shout out to Phil Cousineau who taught me: *Show, don't tell.*

A special thank you to Francis. Thank you for being there each day and for taking me on the road less travelled.

Thank you to my sons, Jared and Jonah Nangle. Jared, thank you for working with me and helping me be a better writer. I know you will *make things.* Jonah, thank you for being who you are. You are my example of courage in life.

To my mother and biggest fan, Edda Ashe. Thank you for making everything easier than it would otherwise be, and for always making me feel like *I can.*

Contents

"The ancestor of every action is a thought."

Ralph Waldo Emerson

Chapter One
THE THOUGHT

Their white lab coats are splattered with so many colors, they look like chefs instead of scientists. The room smells of sulfur. There are glass beakers everywhere, and they are sweaty from too many hours around the lab table. It's not an ideal vision of the afterlife, but it's what Marvin Millet and the other scientists chose when they crossed over.

The scientists meet each day to discuss the living.

"It's a beautiful thing, how thoughts work in the world," one scientist begins.

The contrary scientist squirms in his seat.

"You think that everything is beautiful. But, is there beauty in hatred? How about slow, painful death? There's nothing beautiful about that. I could go on and on. You are deluded into thinking that the world is a beautiful place, when it's not. Clearly not."

"I'm not saying everything is beautiful. I'm simply saying that the thought is a beautiful thing."

"What's so beautiful about it?"

"It has unlimited potential."

The contrary scientist gets up from the lab table and walks around the outside of the group.

"You believe that thoughts are the answer to the world's problems. Thoughts are just thoughts, nothing more than that."

Marvin Millet stands as well, gathering the subjects of their earlier experiment.

"The thought is the seed of everything else. Our thoughts determine how we see the world."

The contrary scientist begins pacing back and forth.

"You're glorifying them."

"Am I? Do you know what thoughts are made of?"

Marvin holds up an empty glass beaker and looks into it, as though it held secrets to the universe.

The contrary scientist is unimpressed.

"I know what you believe."

Marvin looks directly into his eyes.

"Yes, thoughts are filled with boundless energy."

The contrary scientist shakes his head.

"I doubt that's true."

"Well, it is true," Marvin quickly retorts and continues on.

"Our thoughts have power beyond our imagination. They lead to our values and ultimately our actions."

The contrary scientist is unmoved.

"You may believe that thoughts are powerful, but people are struggling as much as they ever have."

Marvin takes off his lab coat, a sign that he's ready to move on.

"We can't change the world overnight. But, when people change their thoughts, they change themselves. And by changing themselves, they change the world."

**The Thought Store: Employee Manual
Section 1a - The Thought**

The thought is the electro-chemical
reaction in the brain that forms ideas,
plans or pictures.

Our thoughts result in our values and
actions.

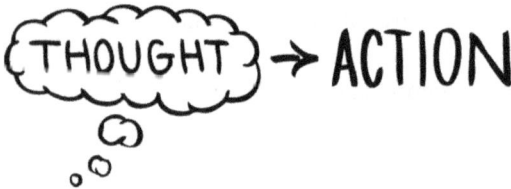

Figure I

We have about 60,000 thoughts a day.

Chapter Two
MARVIN MILLET

One hundred and nine years earlier, Marvin Millet was a young boy fascinated by the world of thoughts. While other kids were playing sports and doing homework, Marvin spent his afternoons studying thought atoms and imagining where his thoughts came from. Even in the year 2306, this was an unusual interest for a child.

Marvin's love of science and thoughts was peculiar to his parents who came from a long line of farmers. "No one in our family likes to think," his father said. "It's a waste of time."

"Dad, you're thinking all the time, whether you realize it or not."

"No, I'm not," his father said indignantly.

Marvin's mother knew that Marvin was different from other children and often said he was born wearing a scientist's smock. For his tenth birthday his parents made it official and bought him a white lab coat. Marvin rarely took it off.

"You can't wear that smock to school," his mother said.

"But, I look really good in it!"

Marvin knew he was a scientist in his bones, and he liked that the coat showed the world who he was. Between the smock, his bushy black hair, and thick black glasses, everyone thought Marvin was ten years older than his age.

"You're in love with thoughts," Marvin's friends teased.

"So what if I am," he replied.

While Marvin's thinking was strong and positive, he worried about his younger brother Julian, who thought quite the opposite. Julian was overwhelmed by a steady stream of low quality, negative thoughts.

Things never go my way. That's the story of my life.
I have the worst luck.

When Marvin was thirteen years old, a science experiment at school got out of hand, resulting in a large explosion that nearly burned down the classroom. Tragically, Marvin lost one of his arms in the accident. Julian knew he could never survive something so awful.

"How do you do it? How did you go through something so terrible and still be OK?"

"I have no idea."

As the boys got older, Marvin's thinking grew stronger, while Julian's thinking got progressively worse.

I'm sick of this. This is killing me.

Until that time, few people had heard of *solidification*. It was a fairly new disease, only a dozen reported cases in ten years, so there wasn't much information. Marvin and his parents had no idea that Julian was experiencing the early symptoms.

Solidification occurs when the body loses too much energy and slows down to the point of becoming solid and immovable like a statue.

Negative thinking is one of the main causes because it drains the body's energy.

One weekend Marvin visited Julian in college and noticed him limping. Julian said that he twisted his ankle, but it was a lie. He limped around for weeks, hoping it would go away, but the solidification was taking hold. Within a month, at twenty-one years of age, Julian solidified in his apartment. When Marvin heard, he was devastated and felt responsible.

How was Julian's thinking so bad, and I didn't know?

Fueled by the loss of his brother, Marvin became a prestigious physicist and pursued his interest in thoughts with even greater passion, looking for anything that would help others avoid Julian's fate. After months of tireless study, Marvin came to a simple conclusion.

Julian needed better thoughts and had no idea how or where to get them.

That's when it hit him.

I'll start a company that sells only the best thoughts!

Marvin could see it. He would open a chain of stores, brick and mortar stores, that displayed the power of thoughts.

When people see how powerful thoughts are, with their own eyes, they'll buy them.

One night, sitting alone in a cafe, he shared his grand idea with the woman next to him, but she was skeptical.

"People can get great thoughts for free. They're everywhere."

"BUT, THEY DON'T!" Marvin blurted in her face.

"When we are unhappy, or stressed, or around bad thinkers, or sick, or if we never learned how to think correctly, then we don't think very well at all."

Soon after, Marvin Millet opened The Thought Store. Eventually, he opened 33,407 retail stores that sold only powerful, life changing thoughts.

The Thought Store: Employee Manual Section 2a – Our Thoughts Have a Vibration.

The vibration of our thoughts affects the body, our emotions, the people around us, and the world we live in.

Figure II

How we think is a habit.

Chapter Three
HENRY GEORGE

Henry George arrives to work. He unlocks the door and turns on the lights. He walks around the room and feels the temperature. It needs to be exactly 68 degrees.

At five minutes before 9:00 Henry releases thousands of thoughts into The Thought Store. He watches them flow from the air vents and drift to the ceiling, forming billowing, buoyant clouds of great thoughts.

The year is 2415.

Henry, a tall, lanky, thirty year old man with warm, brown eyes is the manager of Thought Store #111. When he was hired nine years ago his parents had opposite reactions.

"Henry, that company puts some kind of glue in the thoughts," his mother warned him, "to make them stick better."

"That's ridiculous," his father said. "It's an honor for our son to be selling thoughts."

"It's not an honor to sell something that sticks to your brain!"

Henry never understood his father's passion for thoughts. However, he hoped that by working for The Thought Store, he'd discover their power.

Henry has tried to use the power of thought all of his life. However, it doesn't work for him, he can't do it, and he doesn't like it.

I don't know why I think like I do, but I do.

Growing up, Henry's parents were very different from one another. His mother worried constantly, and his father was positive about everything.

"It's like living under a strobe light," he told his friends.

"Don't they balance each other out?"

"No, they don't."

When Henry was eleven years old, his mother's worrying got so bad that he stopped hearing anything she said. Her voice reached such a loud, terrible pitch that Henry no longer heard the words. All he heard was a bullhorn sound projecting from her mouth.

"Henry, hoooooooooonk!"

In the middle of her bullhorn speech, Henry ran outside and sat under his favorite tree. He imagined having a treehouse to hide in but was afraid of climbing the tree.

Maybe I can build a treehouse under the tree.

However, Henry challenged himself in other ways. In high school he ran for class Secretary and won. He was so nervous about his acceptance speech that he threw up outside the gym. After his speech, a girl approached him.

"Hello, Henry."

Henry just stared at her. Without saying a word, he stood there for over a minute. Not knowing what to do, she walked away.

Why did I do that?

"Henry, courage is being afraid and doing things anyway," his father said.

Maybe I'm braver than I think.

Overall, Henry didn't believe he was brave. He feared death; he feared not being loved; he feared looking foolish; he feared being disfigured or buried alive. Henry spent hours thinking of ways that life could hurt him.

He asked his friends, "Do you ever think about really bad things happening to you?"

"Sometimes, but not usually," they replied.

"Did you hear the story about the girl who fell in a hole and had to breathe through a tube?"

Henry wondered how he could sleep at night while people were lying in holes, breathing through tubes.

He tried to hide his thoughts from his father, but his father was too knowledgeable about thoughts. Henry's father was a leader in the Thought Movement. Their charter was to help people think in ways that made them happier and more successful.

"Henry, there is something I want you to understand: no matter what you hear, it's your thoughts that create your life."

However, Henry didn't believe that was true.

I thought every day about living in a treehouse, under my tree, and that never happened.

Strong thoughts physically lift us.

Chapter Four
SELLING THOUGHTS

Standing in the back of the store, Henry hikes up his loose pants and makes sure the thoughts are displayed correctly. The compassionate thoughts are in the front of the store, near the entrance. The beliefs are next to them, on the right. There are forty thought sections in all.

The Thought Store only sells high quality thoughts, but some customers ask about buying low quality thoughts or *low-vibes* as they are commonly called.

"We don't sell them," Henry answers. "Low-vibes are heavy and customers trip over them. Anyway, we don't want to put more of them into the world."

The first customer of the day arrives shopping for a thought about money.

"What kinds of thoughts about money do you want to have?"

The customer looks down.

"I don't know, but my current thoughts aren't working."

Henry understands quite well.

"I see."

Reviewing his inventory, Henry looks at thoughts for increasing income, thoughts for addressing the fear of not having enough, optimistic thoughts, etc.

"What about: *I'm rich.*"

"No, I'll never believe that thought."

Henry looks at his inventory further.

"How about, *I intend to be paid boatloads of money for sharing my talents and gifts*. That thought calibrates at 353."

She thinks for a moment and smiles at the amusing visual of the thought.

"My thoughts have been measuring closer to 120. That will be a huge boost. I'll take that one."

Customers have twenty-one days to make the thought into a habit. After that they lose the thought. They complain it's not enough time. "Sorry, it's company policy."

The Thought Store principles and practices are outlined in the employee manual, written by Marvin Millet. He wanted to ensure that his research on thoughts was clearly documented for the world to know.

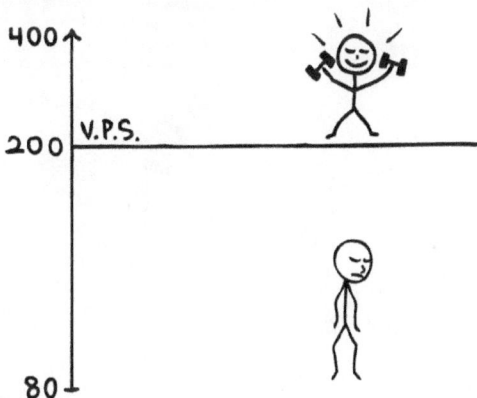

**The Thought Store: Employee Manual
Section 4a – Thoughts Can Be Measured**

Every thought can be measured to determine if it makes the body weak or strong. Thoughts that measure below 200 vibrations per second will lower the body's energy. Thoughts above 200 vibrations per second (v.p.s.) strengthen the body.

Figure IV

I notice what I think about.

Chapter Five
HENRY AND LIFE

Each night when Henry arrives home from work he goes straight to the refrigerator. He loves opening his refrigerator. There is something comforting about the backlit food sitting there, waiting for him.

I like my refrigerator.

Henry likes many things about his life. But, for some reason his good thoughts are constantly bombarded by his weak ones. It's as though his thoughts are at war, and the good thoughts don't stand a chance.

Henry has read dozens of books to understand his life better. One book suggested he shouldn't over think things. So, he tried to think less but couldn't.

Other books told him how to be happy all the time, but Henry doesn't need happiness all the time. He'd be fine with contentment, mild joy, or occasional fulfillment.

Henry is open to advice. That's what people like about him. He's confused but pleasantly so. A friend said to him once:

"Henry, when I'm with you, I feel better about myself."

Great. Henry thought. *I'm glad my confusion makes you feel better.*

Henry realizes he won't be leading large groups of people to the holy grail. He doesn't see himself as a beacon for guiding others. He's fine with that. He doesn't want that much attention.

Henry simply wants to enjoy his life.

One negative thought attracts another;
they are drawn together like magnets.

Chapter Six
THE DOWNWARD SPIRAL

A downturn in the economy is affecting many of the 33,407 Thought Stores. Unfortunately, Henry's store is experiencing one of the largest declines.

"You can't just float the thoughts in front of people anymore."

Henry is called into regional headquarters to discuss his poor sales and he's dreading it. As a child Henry was rarely reprimanded, and when he was, even in the slightest way, it was unbearable for him. When a teacher looked at him sideways or said his name aloud, he wanted to shrink into a tiny ball and roll inconspicuously out the door.

When Henry arrives at Thought Store headquarters, he nervously reads the sign above the main entrance:

> "The only thing standing between you and success
> is your thoughts."
>
> ~ *Marvin Millet*

With a sick feeling in his stomach, Henry walks the long corridor to his meeting.

Just focus on the issues. Be open to what they have to say. I don't need to think about anything else. My truck is making a new sound. How much is that going to cost? Don't think about any of that. Just be confident.

Henry continues down the hallway, looking for the meeting room.

Am I lost? How embarrassing. Did they say room 210 or 310?

Henry walks the maze of hallways hoping that people haven't noticed that he's going in circles.

Who am I kidding? I'm way over my head in this job. I always have been. How will I make a living after they fire me? I'm too old to live with my parents.

The Thought Store: Employee Manual Section 6a – The Downward Spiral From a Negative Thought

The Downward Spiral - When one negative thought leads to another, creating a feeling of hopelessness and despair.

NEGATIVE
THOUGHT

Figure VI

*Our thoughts can be calibrated
for their strength.*

Chapter Seven
THE MEASUREMENT ROOM

In his meeting, Henry reviews his year to date sales and projected revenues for Thought Store #111. Dissatisfied with his performance, management gives him three months to turn things around.

Driving home, Henry stops for lunch at the beach. He makes his way to the sand and finds a flat, clean spot, yards away from anyone else.

What am I going to do?

Henry watches the waves, one by one, rippling onto the shore.

If I weren't selling thoughts, what else would I do?

He looks to the ocean for answers.

I like playing chess. I could be a professional chess player.

He pictures himself on a big stage, sitting in front of a chess board, with hundreds of people watching.

I don't think so.

Henry gets in his truck and drives back to The Thought Store. As he enters the store he looks at the thoughts with sadness, realizing he may not be around them much longer.

I've had nine years to be good at this job ... and I'm not.

The store is empty so Henry opens his mail, a routine he oddly enjoys. Each day employees are sent an excerpt from The Thought Store manual to review. It was a practice Marvin Millet began when he started the company.

Henry reads today's manual excerpt:

**The Thought Store: Employee Manual
Section 7a - The Sum of Our Thoughts**

Since the vibration of our thoughts
affects the vibration of the body, it is
important that all individuals measure
the vibration of their thoughts.

Figure VII

Henry hears a honking horn and nearly falls out of his chair.
Frightened that someone might be reading his thoughts, he
looks around the store to make sure he's alone.

The Thought Store

Henry closes his mail, sits back in his chair and looks sheepishly at the Measurement Room. Every Thought Store has one. The small closet-like room measures how much power there is in a person's thoughts.

The Measurement Room gives the plain, ugly truth. It doesn't sprinkle sugar on it and hand it to you in a pink cupcake. It tells you directly: This is what your thoughts are doing to your life.

Henry hates the Measurement Room, truly hates it, and has never been inside.

～～～

That night Henry dreams about an enormous snake that is slithering on the floor of The Thought Store. The snake comes toward him, gliding slowly, its tongue darting from its mouth. Henry screams inside the store, but no one hears him.

The snake bends its body at a forty-five degree angle and looks Henry directly in the eyes. Staring into the eyes of something so repulsive to him is nearly impossible, but Henry refuses to look away.

"I'm not afraid of you," Henry says.

The snake gives a sly, confident grin.

"Yes, you are."

Most of our thoughts each day are
the same thoughts we had the day before.

Chapter Eight
HENRY MEETS ELLA

The next day, Henry walks the showroom floor, looking up at the thoughts floating, jumping and bouncing in the airspace. Using a large feather-like apparatus called a Butterfly Fan, Henry is rotating the thoughts when a customer walks in. Henry looks toward the door and sees a young, attractive woman with light hair and dark eyes.

"May I help you?"

The woman is visibly nervous, but Henry is accustomed to new customers being uneasy in the store.

"Please let me know if you have any questions."

She's quiet, thinking about her question.

"Do your thoughts really work?"

Henry hears this question every day, and his answer is always the same. However, with this woman he feels compelled to be honest.

"I don't know if they work."

The young woman laughs, her dark eyes sparkling, adding to Henry's embarrassment.

"You work for a store that sells thoughts and you don't know if they work?"

Realizing she is making Henry uncomfortable, she changes the subject and introduces herself.

"My name is Ella."

Henry looks closely at the dark eyed woman. She's different from his regular customers.

"Hello, I'm Henry."

Standing awkwardly before her, Henry wonders what to say next, when she speaks instead.

"Henry, would you like to have dinner with me tonight?"

Thrown by her abrupt invitation, Henry pauses. He's not sure if he's attracted to her or afraid of her.

Ella notices his hesitation.

"You can tell me about working in a store that sells thoughts."

His store is struggling; he feels lost and doesn't know what he's going to do.

"I'm not sure that'll be interesting for you."

"It certainly seems interesting. You get to hear what people are really thinking."

Recalling the thoughts he's heard over the last nine years, Henry smiles.

"That's true. But, people usually think the same thoughts every day."

Henry feels increasingly inadequate.

She's much too attractive for me. She's much too everything for me.

He quickly changes the subject.

"Are you interested in buying a new thought?"

Ella has been considering buying thoughts for some time.

"Maybe, but I doubt they'll work on me."

Surprised that she is doubting herself, Henry is intrigued.

"Why do you say that?"

"Years of experience with myself."

Henry understands perfectly.

Ella spends another ten minutes in the store talking with Henry while reading the many thoughts displayed above her.

"Henry, have any of your customers ever solidified?"

All Thought Store managers are supposed to give the company statement regarding solidification. However, Henry doesn't want to hold anything back.

"We had one customer about a year ago, a woman."

Ella's body feels chilled.

"What did she look like after it happened?"

Henry thinks back and shudders.

"Her face was frozen with the most hopeless expression. They say that your final thought molds onto your face."

Negative thoughts deplete the body.

Chapter Nine
ELLA

Ella returns home and looks in the mirror at a face she thinks is oddly asymmetrical. She gets up and wanders around her home, feeling safe and comfortable there.

At the age of twenty-five Ella is tired of dating. Now, she dreads the boring routine: sounding more interested than she is, asking questions to balance out the conversation, laughing to appear light and pleasant.

But, Henry is different.

I want it to work this time.

With her mind busy reviewing the day, replaying her conversations, Ella makes a cup of coffee. She thinks of a rude person in the check-out line of the grocery store earlier that day. Her mind drifts from one agitating thought to another. It's a habit.

My head hurts. Why didn't Anne call me back? I'm tired of her. Why did I eat so much today? I'm gaining weight. I hope I don't run into Bob at work. I should learn how to play the piano. It's too hard. My hair looks terrible.

Exhausted by her thoughts, Ella takes a breath. She thinks about Henry. There is something inexplicable about him. He's self-conscious and endearing.

He's kind.

That night, Henry and Ella go out to dinner. They talk about their jobs, their dreams, their fears. They share the kind of information people reveal when they want to be known.

After dinner they decide to go to The Passages. The Passages is a place people go for a fun escape or a life altering experience. It consists of long hallways that lead to different experiences. They have names like: Adrenaline, Fear, and Explosion. Henry has no interest in having any of these experiences, but he smiles as he realizes that his attachment to Ella already feels like fear and adrenaline.

He follows her into what appears like the entrance to a cave. They don't have any light to guide them, so they step into the darkness and follow each others voices and body heat.

"Where are we?"

"This passage is called Uncertainty."

They walk about 100 yards down the dark corridor, when Henry notices it's gotten quiet.

"Ella, are you here?"

When she doesn't respond, Henry realizes he is alone. Somehow he's either walked down the wrong passage or Ella has moved too far ahead of him.

How did I lose her? I wanted tonight to go well and now I've lost her in this dark tunnel. Did she lose me on purpose? Is something wrong with her?

The thoughts cascade into one another as Henry reaches for air. He doesn't want to think these thoughts; he was having such a good time. He bends his head back and tries to catch a good clean breath, but the thoughts keep coming.

Things never go my way.
I'm doomed to be alone forever.
It's over.

With that thought, Henry passes out.

**The Thought Store: Employee Manual
Section 9a - FACE: Balancing Feeling
and Thinking ™**

Don't use thoughts to avoid your
emotions. Instead, use thoughts to help
you feel stronger and more confident.
Practice **FACE: Balancing Feeling and
Thinking™** (See Appendix A for detail.)

1. Face your emotions fully.
2. Accept how you feel.
3. Choose a good thought.
4. Exhale.

FACE ACCEPT CHOOSE EXHALE

Figure IX

Our thoughts are reflected in the outside world.

Chapter Ten
LOW-VIBE THOUGHTS

After his humiliation in the Passage, Henry goes for a walk. He made up an excuse for passing out, but doubts Ella believed him. As he's strolling the streets he sees Massive Thoughts, a Thought Store competitor. He's never been in the store and feels compelled to walk inside.

The Thought Store only sells thoughts that are light, airy and cloud-like. Massive Thoughts, on the other hand, sells both high-vibes and low-vibes.

Before entering Massive Thoughts, Henry looks down the sidewalk, carefully left and right, making sure no one sees him. Inside the store, he whispers to the salesperson.

"Excuse me, do you carry any low-frequency thoughts?"

The salesperson responds in a loud, booming voice.

"We have a large selection of dead thoughts. What do you have in mind?"

Henry whispers back, trying to lower the volume of their conversation.

"What did you call them?"

"Dead thoughts, that's just a name I gave 'em. Don't worry, they don't really kill you."

Haven't you heard of solidification?

Henry quickly mumbles three of his own worst thoughts. The salesperson disappears into the back room and releases three low-vibes into the airspace. Henry stands back and watches as the thoughts fall from the air vents and splatter on the floor, soaking Henry's shoes. The salesperson is thoroughly amused by the mucous covered thoughts landing at Henry's feet.

"Sorry about that. It happens."

Annoyed by the salesperson, Henry quickly leaves the store. He runs down the street for over a mile until he's safely in The Thought Store. Closing the door quickly behind him, Henry places both hands on the bar of the door, pushing his body against it like he's being chased.

I can't keep thinking like this.

His hands gripping the bar of the door, Henry looks down at his wet shoes. He takes off his socks to dry out his feet. In the quiet solitude of the store, Henry can hear the faint buzzing sound of the thoughts filed in the back room.

Henry looks at the Measurement Room.

I need to know.

Henry stares at the little room, waiting for human skeletons to emerge, dance around the store and escort him to his death.

I need to know.

He gets up from his chair and walks slowly into the small room. Standing inside, his heart beating furiously, he starts nervously humming.

Hmm. Hmm. Hmm.

Realizing it's time, Henry closes the door and begins thinking. The timer is set for fifteen minutes, the time necessary to get an accurate reading.

I need to know the truth.

Courageously, Henry lets go ... and thinks his normal thoughts.

When limiting beliefs are removed,
we see ourselves clearly.

Chapter Eleven
HENRY'S THOUGHT MEASUREMENT

When Henry steps out of the Measurement Room, he takes a deep breath and reads his thought measurement. He winces as though he's been punched in the stomach.

My thoughts are ...

He quickly ends his thought. He can't afford it now.

Barefooted, Henry roams the showroom floor, unsure of what to do next.

Something has to change. I can't keep thinking the same thoughts year after year.

He looks again at the Measurement Room knowing it's held the secret thoughts of many who've gone before him. He shudders when he thinks of the countless numbers of private, low-vibe thoughts that will follow people to their graves.

Desperate for answers, he scans his mail and finds a manual excerpt from a month ago:

**The Thought Store: Employee Manual
Section 11a – Beliefs Are Thoughts
We Hold Onto.**

Our beliefs tell us what we think is
possible in our lives and in the world. It
is advised that Thought Store employees
go through Belief Optimization annually.

Figure XI

What do I believe?

Henry looks up at the empty ceiling, empty yet filled with
possibility.

What do I believe is possible for me?

He walks into the back room where the thoughts are stored and reviews the beliefs inventory:

I will achieve my goals.
I will have financial independence.
I will find true love with another.
I can make a difference in the world.

Henry reviews dozens of powerful beliefs. However, he doesn't believe any of them.

We all have low quality thoughts,
it's the sum quality of our thoughts that matters.

Chapter Twelve
ELLA'S THOUGHTS

Henry's phone lights up, startling him. He sees that it's Ella and doesn't answer.

Not now. Not right now.

A few minutes later it lights up again. The light flashes so many times that he wonders if it's broken. Unable to ignore it any longer, Henry finally answers.

"Hello Ella."

"Hello Henry."

Preoccupied, Henry is silent.

"Henry, I need to talk to you."

Ella tells Henry the reason she came into The Thought Store that morning. Henry listens anxiously as she tells him how her foot has been numb for weeks, and now the toes on her right foot feel solid, like little stones.

She wants Henry to measure her thoughts.

Frightened for them both, Henry has Ella come in immediately. When she arrives, Henry is nervously waiting by the entrance. They embrace, their date still fresh on their minds; however, the lightness of their initial meeting is gone.

"Henry, are you OK?"

He forces a smile.

"I'm fine, it's been a long day. Are you ready?"

"I'm ready. How long does it take?"

"You have to be inside the Measurement Room for at least fifteen minutes. Most people think only high-vibes for the first minute, hoping they can maintain that level. But, fairly quickly the true nature of a person's thinking kicks in."

"Henry, I appreciate you for doing this. I don't think I'd have the courage if you weren't here."

"Ella, don't worry, we all think terribly sometimes."

"Yes, we do."

She steps inside the Measurement Room, while Henry walks around the side and turns it on.

"OK Ella, relax and think. I'll let you know when you're done."

Inside the room, Ella does her best to think as she normally would and finds that it's easier than expected. The minutes tick by as Ella becomes lost in her thoughts.

Henry is increasingly nervous. A person's thought measurement is a private matter. He'd rather not know. Ten minutes pass, leaving five minutes to go. There is a small window into the room, but Henry can't bring himself to look inside. As the minutes go by, Henry feels worse.

The buzzer finally sounds, signifying that fifteen minutes are over.

Thank goodness, hopefully her number isn't too low and this whole thing will blow over.

Henry opens the door to the Measurement Room and finds Ella lying on the floor in a puddle of thick, heavy thoughts. In nine years of measuring thoughts this hasn't happened. Disoriented, Ella opens her eyes.

"What is this?"

Panicked by the sight of Ella's thoughts spreading like lava across the floor, Henry answers.

"These are your thoughts in physical form."

Ella carefully places her finger in the thick, glutenous thoughts, then quickly pulls it away.

"What did they measure at?" Ella asks, hesitantly.

Henry gives her a number, but it's a lie. He can't bring himself to tell her the true measurement of her thoughts.

Our beliefs tell us what is possible.

Chapter Thirteen
HOT BELIEFS

Henry knows that he and Ella must act quickly. They are losing energy with every thought that oozes through their bodies.

He tells Ella the truth. He tells her the true measurement of her thoughts. He tells her the measurement of his own thoughts. He tells her that he's struggled with his thinking for most of his life.

"Ella, we are losing too much energy. We have to do something to reverse things."

Ella quickly notes her dead toes, checking them constantly for any movement.

"What can we do?"

"There's a place called *Hot Beliefs*. They help you see which of your beliefs are ... hurting you."

Ella hates the idea, stone-like toes or not.

"Henry, if one more person tells me to believe in myself, to believe I can do anything, to believe and believe and it will be OK, I'm going to scream."

It's been a long day, and Henry is losing patience.

"Ella, they say it helps you see yourself clearly."

"Why would I want to see myself clearly? If I don't like what I see, the last thing I want is to see it clearly!"

Exhausted, Henry listens as Ella continues.

"Henry, why are you struggling? If you're such an expert at thinking and seeing things clearly ... why do you think as you do?"

Henry wonders about the same thing, every day.

"I don't know. But, I know it's not good."

Ella notes her dead toes again, then moves the toes on her other foot, wondering if they'll harden as well.

"OK ... we should go in the morning."

First thing the next day they go to *Hot Beliefs*, the largest belief optimization company in the United States. Ella arrives looking worse than the night before.

"I barely slept," she says plainly.

"Either did I."

When they enter *Hot Beliefs*, the person in charge guides them into a small work area with a table and two chairs. A large screen covers one wall.

"How does this work?" Henry asks the attendant.

"First, we perform a lobotomy."

The attendant laughs, making Henry and Ella even more uncomfortable.

"No, of course not! You are going to watch a short film with sensors attached to your pulse points. While you're viewing the film, you will be unconsciously thinking about the possibilities for your life. Our system extracts those beliefs. When the film is over, you'll be given the list of what they are."

Ella looks sideways at Henry.

"Afterward, you can go over to The Thought Store and buy new beliefs."

Henry is too embarrassed to tell him that he works for The Thought Store.

They attach the sensors and watch the film. It runs for ten minutes and is filled with contrasting themes of love and hate, joy and pain, and success and failure.

When it is over, the man in charge hands them both their list of detrimental beliefs in a confidential envelope. They open their envelopes and read down the list. When Henry finishes his list, he looks at Ella who is still reading hers. When she finally finishes, she turns to Henry.

"Henry, this is too much. I can't do this."

Looking closely at Ella, Henry wishes he could jump inside her head and think for her, if only for a moment.

"Ella, what do you ..."

Henry fumbles with his words, knowing that the *b* word is one he probably shouldn't be using right now.

"Ella, what do you *think* is possible for you?"

Staring down at the ground, Ella doesn't say a word.

"Ella!" Henry continues, raising his voice as though speaking louder will help. "What do you *think* is possible in your life?"

Looking fragile, as though a small breeze could knock her to the ground, Ella whispers:

"Henry, I honestly don't know."

Walking along the street in front of *Hot Beliefs*, Henry and Ella walk in silence. Ella tries desperately to reverse her thoughts, knowing that every thought is hurting her.

"Are you OK?" Henry asks, feebly.

"No, I'm not."

Henry walks quietly beside her. To him it looks like nothing more than this. However, Ella is spiraling downward as she's experienced countless times before. This time she is unable to stop the steady flow of painful thoughts being pumped through her system.

I can reverse my thoughts at any time.

Chapter Fourteen
THE QUANTUM LADDER

The Quantum Ladder is a gigantic ladder the height of a ten-story building and as wide as a football field. It was built to help people restore their lost energy. Realizing that Ella is becoming weaker with each thought, Henry takes her there immediately. When they arrive, they are greeted by an old man with a long, gray beard who reminds Henry of his grandfather. The old man welcomes them and explains how the ladder works.

"As you climb the ladder your energy is replenished. However, you cannot have any low-vibes while on the ladder, or you'll fall."

Henry weighs the risk and fears it's too difficult. However, he's hesitant to argue with a man who looks like he's lived forever.

"Sir, we are here because she can't maintain higher thoughts!"

"She has to hold the good thoughts long enough for the ladder to restore her energy. That's how it works."

"I don't understand!" Henry protests. "Look at her! How is she supposed to think high frequency thoughts when she feels like this?"

The old man responds patiently. He hears this question every day.

"It's OK that she feels bad. Her feelings won't kill her. It's her thoughts that are the problem, I assure you."

Realizing it's time to climb the ladder, Henry accepts what the old man says.

"Thank you, sir. Come on, Ella, we'll do this together."

The first rung of the ladder is 20 feet off the ground, without a net below. Henry and Ella walk towards the foot of the ladder. Standing beneath it, Henry runs over in his mind what to do. He looks at Ella and though she is expressionless, tears are forming in her eyes.

Henry urges Ella to climb the leg of the ladder as Henry follows. They place their feet in the indentations along the ladder's leg and slowly make their way to the first rung.

"Ella, I know how hard this is, but please deactivate any low-vibes right now. Think of something that makes you feel good."

Ella is silent. She stares at the rung with such intensity that Henry is sure she will be able to make it and move on.

"Ella please, only good thoughts."

Tears are streaming down Ella's face.

"You can do this."

Ella shifts her weight from the leg of the ladder and reaches for the first rung. Looking at her from the side of the ladder, Henry holds his breath.

Jumping towards the rung of the ladder like a trapeze artist, Ella attempts to grasp it with both hands, but one hand misses. Dangling from the first rung, Ella tries with all of her strength to pull herself up.

"Ella, hold on!"

Ella loses her grip and lets go. In a singular moment, Ella's young, beautiful body solidifies and falls. Henry jumps from the leg of the ladder to catch her and falls as well. Both of them drop quickly to the ground and smash against the pavement. As they hit, Ella's body breaks into pieces and Henry passes out. Other people standing by cover their ears to a crashing sound, like plates shattering against a wall.

When Henry awakes he is lying next to Ella's broken body, a mosaic of stones scattered along the ground. Henry is suddenly aware that he is there, and she is not. Although his body survived the fall, he feels as though someone has grabbed him by the throat and is suffocating him.

He looks one last time at Ella, hoping to see the beautiful face he remembers from just days ago. Instead she looks old and tired, her final thoughts etched onto her face.

The Thought Store: Employee Manual Section 14a - The Power of Low-Vibe Thoughts

Low-vibe thoughts are dangerous. Whether we think them in small or large amounts, low frequency thoughts drain the potential from our lives.

Figure XIV

We can change our lives,
by changing our thoughts.

Chapter Fifteen
BACK AT THE LAB

From the lab, Marvin Millet watched Henry and Ella fall from the Quantum Ladder, and there was nothing he could do. At times like these, he questions whether his work has made any difference.

"The human body is losing its resistance to agitating thoughts. The rising rates of solidification are staggering."

The scientists nod in agreement.

The contrary scientist steps in, arriving late and taking his lab coat from the closet.

"It's hopeless. I don't see how much longer they can go on."

"People are resilient," Marvin disagrees.

The contrary scientist joins them at the lab table.

"I'm not so sure."

Marvin refrains from leaping out of his chair.

"The human brain can be changed. By altering their thinking habits, people can change their brains."

"But they won't! Most people won't change how they think."

Marvin jumps up from the lab table and stands face to face with the contrary scientist.

"How do you know what people will and won't do?"

The contrary scientist moves closer to Marvin, their noses nearly touching.

"I've watched people think for hundreds of years. There's been little progress."

Calming down and speaking in a slow, steady voice, the conviction of many years of research behind him, Marvin moves even closer.

"That's not true. People are changing their lives by changing their thoughts."

The contrary scientist steps back, puts on his lab coat and turns his attention to the day's preparation.

"We'll see."

The other scientists change the subject.

"How's Henry doing?"

Marvin walks away from the contrary scientist.

"He's having a hard time. He knows he needs to change the way he thinks, but doesn't believe he can."

"Ah, self-doubt is a problem."

"Yes, a serious problem."

"Maybe we should create a manual for them. It would make their time easier."

"No, no, no! That's a terrible idea!"

Marvin steps in authoritatively.

"For Henry to change his thinking, he needs to change his habits."

The lab is quiet, waiting for Marvin's next words.

"If he doesn't change his thinking, nothing will change in his life."

"It's true," they chime in unison.

Worried for Henry, Marvin paces the floor.

"The *8 Simple Thinking Habits* are clearly stated in the Thought Store manual, but he's not interested in learning them."

There is power in repetition.

Chapter Sixteen
REPETITION

Henry is struggling. Ella meant something to him, and she's gone. It happened so fast. However, with less than three months to turn things around at The Thought Store and the fear of solidification, Henry must act swiftly. He turns to his daily manual excerpt.

The Thought Store: Employee Manual Section 16a - The Brain

Our thoughts and lifestyle habits are creating new pathways in the brain. As thinking habits change through repetition, picture the pathway in the brain becoming a major highway.

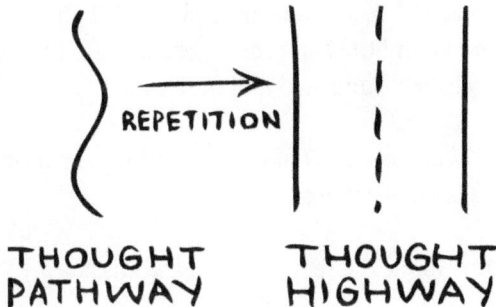

THOUGHT PATHWAY

THOUGHT HIGHWAY

Figure XVI

Henry thinks back to his date with Ella in the Passages. He remembers a Passage called: Repetition.

With his low thought measurement flashing in his mind like a caution sign, Henry heads over to the Passages. As he walks in he thinks of Ella the night she solidified.

It could happen to anyone. It could happen to me.

He opens the door to the Passage. Inside, Henry sees a large circular path covered in tall, thick grasses and weeds. If Henry can make it through the tall grasses, he'll receive a reward at the start.

Walking as quickly as he can around the weeded path, Henry parts the thick brush with the back of his arms, and stomps over it with his feet. Each time around the path, he treads exactly where he did the last time to get the benefit of the grasses he's already squashed and flattened.

OK, *I get it. This passage is about repetition. The more I do something, the easier it gets.*

Feeling utterly alone, Henry yells into the Passage.

"THIS DOESN'T MATTER! IT'S FAKE! THIS IS A GAME!"

A swift wind blows through the Passage.

"This isn't fake."

Unconvinced, Henry shouts back.

"Does the brain really work like this? Can I really change how I think by repeating thoughts?"

Henry looks down at the weeded path. The grasses are slowly bouncing back.

"Yes, you can."

The Passage hovers over Henry.

"Henry, why did you come here?"

Swallowing his saliva, Henry takes a deep breath.

"I don't want to lose my job."

"Is that why you came? To keep your job?"

"It's not the only reason."

Henry knows the full reason.

"My thoughts are useless, powerless. They're leading me nowhere ..."

Henry's voice trails off and he hears:

"Thoughts have power. Choose them wisely and repeatedly."

Another breeze enters the Passage, rustling Henry's hair.

Thoughts have power. Choose them wisely and repeatedly.

He continues walking the path, stepping where he's stepped before. The grasses begin to whither, the emerald greens turning to gray. As Henry walks the path, he thinks about his life. He runs through his mind the many thoughts that have caused him pain and suffering.

Choose your thoughts wisely and repeatedly.

Will it really matter?

Instantly, the ground tremors and shakes as the Passage descends into the earth, transforming into a circular staircase that enters a dark well.

What is happening? Please tell me what is going on.

The Passage is silent, leaving Henry with only his thoughts. Henry makes his descent, stepping down the staircase until he reaches a platform at the bottom.

With barely enough light to see a door on the landing, Henry reaches for the door knob, then stops.

I don't know where I am. I don't know what I'll find. I don't know if I should.

Hesitantly, Henry turns the handle and slowly opens the door. As it opens, bright light bursts through, knocking Henry to the ground. Stumbling back to his feet, he looks out the door and sees a large pool of water inside a grove of tall, majestic trees. People are laughing and playing in the water, unaware that Henry is present.

Why is this here? Why am I here?

Standing on the landing, looking out at the scene of people and trees, Henry is taken with its beauty and simplicity.

This is one of the most beautiful places I've ever seen.

Watching the people play in the water, Henry can't help but wonder what they are thinking.

Are they thinking at all?

Mesmerized by the sunny, ethereal scene, Henry feels peaceful and at ease.

If only I could feel this way all the time. I'd stay here forever.

In that moment the earth shakes again, this time more violently. The sunny scene disappears and Henry is back in the Passage, on the weeded path where he began. He hears within the Passage:

"*If only* is a worthless thought."

Henry shouts back:

"I'VE HAD PLENTY OF THOSE!"

The Passage responds firmly.

"It's your decision."

Henry is outraged by the suggestion.

"I DON'T PURPOSELY THINK LIKE THIS!"

The Passage is steady and unwavering.

"No, but it's a habit, a pattern."

Henry sits on the ground. His legs are tired. His mind is racing.

Exactly, a habit I can't break.

Henry hears three small words spoken clearly and distinctly.

"Yes, you can."

Mystified that the Passage is reading his private, innermost thoughts, Henry delves deeper.

"How do you know? How do you know if I can?"

The Passage makes one last attempt.

"Because it can be done. Old habits can be broken, and new habits can be learned."

With these words reverberating inside the Passage, Henry whispers:

"Maybe."

Henry feels a sudden tap on his shoulder. He jumps up, turns around and sees no one. Instantaneously, a thought flashes in his mind. It's a thought that's been roaming in the background of Henry's life for years, but Henry ignored it. Now here it is, bold and strong, tapping Henry on the shoulder.

8 Simple Thinking Habits.

Henry looks around the Passage again.

Yes, yes.

The *8 Simple Thinking Habits* were written by Marvin Millet almost a century ago to help people use the power of thought.

Quickly leaving the Passage, with too much adrenaline to drive, Henry runs back to The Thought Store. His long, lanky body runs about a mile until he catches his reflection in a storefront window. Unable to look away, he stares at himself for a long moment.

I can.

Sprinting the last few blocks, Henry arrives at The Thought Store. He swings open the door, expecting the thoughts to rush out and greet him. Immediately, he goes to his desk, opens The Thought Store manual and turns to Appendix A. There he finds what he's looking for:

8 Simple Thinking Habits

Henry starts with the first habit:

"I notice my thoughts."

Henry reads into the night, reading and rereading all eight thinking habits until he falls asleep.

The next day he reads them again.

The day after that he does the same, continuing each day until the *8 Simple Thinking Habits* become habits of his own.

"There is tremendous power in thinking:
I can. I will."

Marvin Millet

Chapter Seventeen
HENRY AND HIS THOUGHTS

Three years later, Henry arrives at Thought Store #111. He unlocks the door, turns on the lights and feels the temperature. It is exactly 68 degrees.

Perfect.

His phone lights up with a call from his mother.

"Henry, you forgot to call me. How can you work for a company that sells thoughts and forget so many of them?"

And why do you call me first thing in the morning and accuse me of something?

Henry notices his thought, takes a breath and chooses another.

I won't let her bullhorn voice upset my morning.

"Sorry about that. I got busy."

Getting off the phone quickly, Henry turns to his mail and sees a message from his manager.

Henry,

We'd like you to speak at our national sales conference next month. Please talk about the key to your success.

I haven't spoken in front of people in a long time.

Henry notices his hesitation, sits with it for a moment and chooses another thought.

It's OK. I'll be prepared, and it'll go great.

His phone lights up a few more times, the third call from a dissatisfied customer.

It's one of those mornings.

"The thought you sold me last week hasn't worked. I've been thinking it over and over and nothing is happening. Your thoughts don't work."

Henry's heart starts to race. He remembers this customer.

I spent over an hour with you trying out different thoughts! What an ungrateful ...

He catches himself.

I don't like this guy.

He catches himself again and smiles, noticing how angry he is at this small, very small situation. He simply notices.

It's OK that I'm angry. I tried to help him.

Henry takes a deep breath.

"I'm sorry sir. If you can come back in, we'll find you a better thought."

"I don't want a better thought and I don't want to drive back in there."

Henry observes his own anger as the heat of emotion moves throughout his body. He lets himself be angry, but doesn't dwell there.

Breathe.

He breathes, reminding himself that angry thoughts will make him more angry. He chooses some high-vibe thoughts instead.

I'm good at my job. I'm having a great day. I can do this. Next!

As Henry's anger subsides, he finds an acceptable solution for the customer, and turns his attention to a new customer who enters the store.

"May I help you?"

"Yes, I'm wondering, do your thoughts really work?"

Henry responds with certainty, explaining how thoughts work in the body and their twenty-one day policy to make the thought into a habit.

That night when the store is closed, Henry gives himself time to *not think*, to be still and quiet. Although he's tempted to move on to the next thing he has to do, he doesn't. Instead, he stops, knowing his mind needs rest.

Sitting in his chair, eyes closed, Henry notices the many thoughts running through his mind, steady and unyielding. He knows how the mind loves to think. In this moment he observes the thoughts coming and going, with his awareness on his breath.

After a short time, Henry turns to his speech.

How I became a top selling Thought salesman.

He thinks about his time with Ella and how she solidified on the Quantum Ladder. He remembers almost losing his job. Looking back, he's painfully reminded of how his thoughts used to sabotage every area of his life.

Writing into the night, Henry enjoys the catharsis of telling his story. He writes a succinct, compelling talk for the conference next month.

When the conference date arrives, Henry is nervous. His fear of public speaking has been with him since his acceptance speech in high school, when he threw up outside the gym.

It's OK. I'm not that kid anymore.

Relying on his thinking habits, Henry doesn't let his nerves take over. He notices that he's nervous, paying attention to any tension in his body. He accepts that he's nervous and breathes. Then, he adjusts his thoughts accordingly.

I can do this. I'll deliver a great speech.

Henry takes a deep breath, letting his nervousness move throughout his body. Next, he chooses thoughts that mean something to him, thoughts that empower him.

I'm sharing my personal story. There is no one better to tell my story than me.

He takes another long, deep breath, notices his lingering nerves and chooses one more thought to put him at ease.

I am relaxed and calm.

It's time. Henry steps up on stage.

Henry tells his story. He recounts the events leading up to his time in the Passage.

"I realized," Henry pauses, knowing what he's about to say is important. "I could change what I think about and how I think, by learning new thinking habits. That decision changed my life."

The audience stands and applauds while Henry looks out at the ocean of people. He remembers sitting on the beach three years ago, looking out at a different ocean, wondering what he would do next.

That feels like so long ago.

As Henry is preparing to leave, he receives a call from his wife.

"How did it go?"

"Hi honey, it went great."

"I'm so happy for you."

The first time Henry saw his wife, she was in line at the grocery store. By that time, Henry had been practicing the *8 Simple Thinking Habits* for over a year, so he was in the habit of noticing his thoughts and adjusting them. He remembers that day like it was yesterday.

She won't be interested in me.

He noticed his thought.

Is that true?

He realized it may not be true and chose another thought.

She might be interested. There's only one way to find out.

"They need to open a line for people who want to buy just one thing," Henry said, playfully.

She looked at him and laughed.

"I know what you mean. I never know what I'll want to eat tomorrow."

They talked in line, through the checkout, in front of the store and into the evening. They weren't dating long before they ultimately married. That was two years ago.

"I'm glad your speech went well. See you when you get home."

"OK, I won't be long," Henry says, eagerly.

On his way home, Henry stops by The Thought Store with something important he needs to do. Walking immediately into the back room, Henry releases the thoughts into the airspace. Watching them gravitate toward one another in their usual fashion, Henry respectfully acknowledges them.

"Thank you."

The thoughts continue bubbling and floating in the air, coaxing Henry to join them. Bouncing off of one another, one of his favorite thoughts catches his eye as he reads it aloud:

"How I think is a habit."

He's heard this thought his entire life.

It's true.

Henry smiles, grateful to be working for a company that sells thoughts: unlimited, powerful, magnificent thoughts.

Appendix A

8 Simple Thinking Habits

1. I notice my thoughts.

2. I ask myself if what I'm thinking about is true.

3. I choose good thoughts throughout the day.

4. I feel my emotions without dwelling on them.

5. I regularly take a break from thinking.

6. I don't look for ways to be offended.

7. I ask for help when I need it.

8. I think of what I'm grateful for at the start of each day.

Thinking Habit # 1

I notice my thoughts.

My thoughts affect every area of my life. What I think about and how I think, demands my attention. The simple act of paying attention to my thoughts is extremely powerful. When I notice my thoughts, I am more aware of what is driving my life.

I notice how my thoughts feel in my body. When I think of something good, I notice that I feel light, warm, energetic and peaceful. When I think: I am beautiful, or I am intelligent, it lifts my energy.

High quality thoughts feel way different in my body than low quality thoughts. With low quality thoughts, I feel heavy and weighed down. Thoughts like: I'm not that smart, or I'm always a mess, make me feel so tired that I want to drop to the ground and sleep.

I notice how my thoughts affect the people around me. I notice how my thoughts influence my emotions. I notice what results I am producing with my thoughts. I am paying attention.

All of this noticing is not a burden. The more I pay attention to my thoughts, the easier it gets. Paying attention moves me one step closer to having my thoughts work for me, not against me.

Thoughts for Thinking Habit # 1

I pay attention to what I'm thinking about.
I notice what I'm creating with my thoughts.
I notice what I'm grateful for.
I am paying attention to the good that is flowing into my life.
I cancel all negative thoughts.
I cancel negative stories I tell myself.
I don't stand in the way of another's path on this earth.
I take responsibility for my words and actions.
I enjoy good thoughts.
I am noticing what is.
I do not try to control other people.
I let go of having to be right.
I focus my thoughts on the best possible outcome.
I notice when my thoughts are heavy.
I notice when my thoughts are light.
I notice when my thoughts feel good.
I notice when my thoughts feel bad.

Thinking Habit # 2

I ask myself if what I'm thinking about is true.

When I am having negative thoughts, I ask myself: What am I thinking about? Is it true? I know that sometimes I have myself upset and worked up over a thought that is not at all true.

When I assume, I make huge leaps in my thoughts. i.e.: My friend didn't call me back: I'm not important enough. My coworker didn't smile at me: she must be angry.

When I worry, I think the worst will happen. i.e.: My son is late: he had an accident. I got dizzy: I have a serious disease.

When I exaggerate, I blow things out of proportion and use words like always and never. These words are usually not true. i.e.: You always do that. I never get it right.

As small as these thoughts are, they create stress and anxiety. It is insanity to be stressed and anxious over a thought that isn't even true!

I will not spend my time thinking about things that haven't happened and are not going to happen. When I notice that my thoughts are negative, I stop and ask myself: What am I thinking about? Is it true?

Thoughts for Thinking Habit # 2

I do not assume people are mad at me.
I do not make assumptions based on very little information.
I pay attention to when I'm being too sensitive.
I do not focus my attention on what can go wrong.
I envision the best possible result.
I cancel negative thoughts.
I know it will be all right.
I prepare to a point, and then I let go.
I am willing to look at what I'm afraid of.
I cancel all untrue, fearful thoughts and stories.
I am learning from the past.
I never underestimate the power of my thinking.
I remain open.
I say what is true for me.
I know that words matter.
I look at situations with a clear mind.
I do not exaggerate because it feels false.
I avoid making uneducated assumptions.
I avoid generalizing because it's usually inaccurate.
I am letting go of worrying because it wastes my energy.
Instead, I educate myself and take action.

Thinking Habit # 3

I choose good thoughts throughout the day.

Because thoughts have energy, I know my thoughts either lift me up or weigh me down; make me weak or make me strong. That's how thoughts work.

I am not a victim of whatever feeling happens to enter my body. I am not subject to the ever-changing conditions around me. I will not be discouraged by the constant chaos that is part of life. That is the power of thought. That is the power of the mind to use thought.

When I feel stressed, I think of something that relaxes me and puts life in perspective. When I am angry, I choose compassionate thoughts that help me through. When I feel unlucky, I choose thoughts that help me feel fortunate. When I am afraid, I choose thoughts that give me courage. When I feel rejected, I choose thoughts that help me feel loved and cared for. When I'm feeling grief, I choose thoughts of self-love and compassion. When I've been hurt, and I feel ready, I choose thoughts of forgiveness. When I am lonely, I choose thoughts that remind me how much I belong.

I choose thoughts that resonate with me and lift me up; thoughts that empower me, and remind me of the unlimited possibilities in my life.

Thoughts for Thinking Habit # 3

I feel good.
I can do this.
I know good things are on the way.
I am healthy and strong.
I am on the right path.
I will get through this.
I forgive those who have hurt me.
I feel loved and cared for.
I am willing to adapt.
I attract great people into my life.
I am determined.
I am grateful for what I have.
I'm right where I need to be.
My life is precious to me.
I enjoy this.
I am honest with myself.
I am relaxed and calm.
I allow what is great in me to come forward.
I have enough energy and talent to do this.
I am grateful to my body for carrying me.
I am grateful to my mind for empowering me.
I believe in myself.
I attract the right opportunities.
I cancel negative thoughts and stories.
I forgive you.
I forgive myself.
I send you peace.
I send myself peace.
I send us both peace.

Thinking Habit # 4

I feel my emotions
without dwelling on them.

I know that my painful feelings won't subside, until I feel them. They aren't going anywhere! Therefore, when I am angry, I don't stuff it down. When I'm sad, I let myself be sad. When I'm afraid, I face my fear. I do not avoid my feelings for two big reasons: One, it doesn't work. And two, the only way to heal my heart, is to feel.

I trust this. I know that nature designs us to heal. I know that if I allow myself to feel whatever emotion arises, I will be able, at some point, to let it go.

I know that my thoughts have an energetic quality to them. I know thoughts are energy.

I know that my thoughts have the power to physically help me in difficult times.

While I don't use thoughts to avoid feeling, I use my thoughts to strengthen and guide me.

I am free of the pain of my past. I am free. I am healing my heart, completely and fully. I know that by allowing myself to feel, I will heal; thereby opening myself to the true power of my thoughts.

Thoughts for Thinking Habit # 4

I do not avoid what I'm feeling.
I respect what is hurt within me.
I have compassion for myself.
I am free of my past.
I allow what I am feeling completely and fully.
I believe that I am healing my heart.
I attract bright white, healing light.
I believe that while my past is part of me, it doesn't define me.
I allow myself to move forward.
I cancel negative thoughts.
I choose to be happy.
I release the pain from my past.
I do not hold onto painful emotions.
I do not indulge painful feelings.
I think of what I am creating with my thoughts.
I feel good.
I will get through this.
I love myself.
I am cleansed of my fear.
I believe in my own strength.
I am committed to growing.
I am learning.
I believe in myself and my ability to move on.
I do not judge my emotions.
I am healing my mind, body and spirit.

FACE:
Balancing Feeling and Thinking ™

1. Face your emotion fully.
2. Accept how you feel.
3. Choose a good thought.
4. Exhale.

1. To face my emotions, I begin by noticing: Am I sad? Angry? Afraid? I notice where the feeling is in my body. Is it in my chest, stomach, or throat? I say to myself: I am angry. I am sad. I am afraid. I use wording that feels accurate for me. I let myself feel. I don't avoid it. I don't hold on. I let the emotion be, without making it more or making it less.

2. Next, I accept that I feel this way. I say: It's OK that I'm afraid. It's OK that I'm angry. I accept that I feel this way. I don't judge myself for feeling.

3. I choose thoughts that strengthen me.
4. I breathe throughout.

EXAMPLE:
Face it fully: I am sad that I lost ... I notice <u>where</u> it is in my body. I notice <u>how it feels</u>. I let myself feel.

Accept it: I accept that I am sad. I do not judge myself. It's OK that I'm sad.

Choose: "I'm ready to feel lighter. I allow myself to move forward. I am strong enough. I am not alone. I am focused on what's working right. I am grateful."

Exhale: I breathe to cleanse the body and mind.

Thinking Habit # 5

I regularly take a break from thinking.

I know that my mind requires rest every day.
When my mind gets overworked, my brain shows
unhealthy signs of stress. When I allow my mind to
not think, I allow inspiration, ideas, and guidance to
come in. When I rest my mind, I gain access to more
clarity; I connect with myself more deeply; and I
increase my brain's ability to heal and function.

I practice not thinking in various ways; one of them
is through meditation. In meditation, when a thought
arises, and they do constantly, I notice the thought
and come back to the present by focusing on my
breath. I am not discouraged by my wandering mind.
I am not discouraged by my constant thinking,
worrying, judging. I notice these thoughts and I
continually come back to my breath.

I practice not thinking by being in the present
moment. It doesn't matter what I'm doing or where I
am. In this place, I don't worry about the future or
focus on the past. I am aware only of what is
happening in the present moment. I practice not
thinking by engaging in activities that bring me closer
to myself and the world around me. It is being in
nature, playing, listening to music I love, or any place
where I feel peaceful and without ego, that I feel
closest to my true being, and my deepest sense of I
am.

Thoughts for Thinking Habit # 5

I am relaxed and at ease.
I am aware of how my mind wanders.
I am aware of where my mind wanders to.
I am able to come back to my breath.
I enjoy resting my mind.
I feel calm and at peace.
I enjoy breathing.
When I breathe, I am filling my body with healing light.
I am listening.
I have compassion for myself.
I enjoy feeling at peace.
I do not judge my steady stream of thoughts.
I allow my thoughts to come and go.
I focus my awareness on my breath.
I notice the sounds in the room.
I notice how my body feels.
I allow my mind to rest.
My mind is healthy and strong.
I care for my mind like I do my body.
I am aware of what I'm feeling.
I am aware of what I'm thinking.

Thinking Habit # 6

I don't look for ways to be offended.

Life offers many, many opportunities to be offended. It is easy to be hurt because people don't always act the way I'd like them to. Situations don't always play out to my advantage. Sometimes, I feel like a target, and people are throwing darts in my direction.

However, I will not spend my life being hurt by the words and actions of others. Sometimes it is intended, more often it is not. It doesn't matter! Either way, I choose how to think about it. It is always my choice.

Therefore, when something happens that could possibly offend me, I take a deep breath and adjust my thoughts so that I will not be offended. This pause gives me a moment to make a deliberate choice of what to think.

I choose to think this way out of respect for myself! I choose to think this way out of preservation for myself! I choose to think this way because I don't have any idea what is in the minds of others and I won't make assumptions. That's not my job.

I will not spend my valuable time and energy being offended by the words and actions of others.

Next!

Thoughts for Thinking Habit # 6

This isn't about me.
I will not be offended by this.
There are issues involved here that I don't understand.
I speak honestly and directly when someone has hurt me.
Then, I let myself feel, and let it go.
Not everything is about me.
This doesn't matter to me.
Other people have their own agendas.
I don't understand people sometimes.
I forgive those who have treated me badly.
I am letting this go.
When there is a problem, I take responsibility for my role in it.
I won't let this ruin my day.
I am hurt, but I'm not dwelling on it.
I pay attention to how others respond to me.
I do not take things personally.
I realize that people have their own issues.
I realize that I have my own issues.
I realize that sometimes people are inconsiderate, but I am not offended by their behavior.
I do not dwell on the inconsiderate behavior of others.
I know that sometimes I am inconsiderate.
I cancel negative thoughts and stories.
I take a deep breath when I am hurt or angry.
I wish you peace.
I wish myself peace.
I with us both peace.

Thinking Habit # 7

I ask for help when I need it.

When I have tried everything, and given all I have, and life still isn't working, I ask for help. At times like these I think: I don't have all the answers. I cannot do this by myself.

First, I exhaust all of my options. I use all of my resources. I dig deep. After I have done all I can do, if I have not succeeded, I ask for help.

I realize that while I have an inner knowing, I may not see clearly all the time. I think: Who or what can help me?

I think of all the resources available to me. I think of where I need to look. Where do I need to turn my attention to get the help I need?

Asking for help involves letting go. I'm letting go of being in control. I am letting go of appearing like I have it all together. I am letting go of being right all the time. I am letting go of being perfect. I am letting go of not being perfect.

These thoughts humble me. They remind me that while I have great potential, and the ability to go to the limits of my imagination, I still need help and guidance along the way.

Thoughts for Thinking Habit # 7

I am letting go.
I am open to the intelligence around me.
I am resourceful.
I am giving all that I can.
I am listening.
I know where to get the help I need.
I know where to get the answers I need.
I realize this is an abundant universe.
I am open to receiving abundance.
I don't have all the answers and that's OK.
I am humble.
I listen to advice when I ask for it.
I hear what others have to say.
I am not closed off to the wisdom around me.
I am open and willing.
I love learning new things about life.
I love learning new things about myself.
As I learn, I grow.
When I let go, answers flow to me.

Thinking Habit # 8

I think of what I'm grateful for at the start of each day.

Each morning, before I get out of bed, I think of everything I am grateful for. This habit reminds me that while life is challenging, I can always find something or someone to be grateful for.

Some days the list is longer than others. But, I always have a list. The more my gratitude becomes an ingrained way of thinking, the longer my list.

When I am grateful, I'm not afraid. When I am grateful, I forget to be mad. When I am grateful, I feel good. When I am grateful, I am letting the universe know that I am paying attention to all that I have.

I don't focus my thoughts on what is wrong. I don't focus my thoughts on what I have lost. Even though I feel the pain of what I've lost, I don't dwell there in my thoughts.

On days when life is difficult, I get down to basics. I am grateful for seeing the sky. I am grateful for my hairy dog. I am grateful for what I can do. When I get down to the basics of what it means to be grateful, I feel joy. My gratitude makes me feel good. When I feel good, I have more to give.

Thoughts for Thinking Habit # 8

I am grateful for all I have.
I am grateful for the people in my life.
I am grateful that I am learning each day.
I am grateful for the parts of my body that work well.
I do not focus on what I've lost.
However, I allow myself to feel what I've lost.
I do not compare my journey to others.
My life is precious to me.
I am grateful for the temporary nature of life.
It's OK that sometimes I think more gratitude than I feel.
I intend to do my best.
I take responsibility for my thoughts and actions.
I trust my thoughts will take me where I need to go.
I enjoy my life.
I accept that life is always changing.
I believe that good things are coming my way.
I am grateful for the kindness of others.
I am grateful for a good night's sleep.
I am grateful for the help I receive.
I am grateful that I keep going.
I intend to be part of creating a better world.

Examples of low-vibe, unhealthy thoughts to avoid:

I'm sick of this.
This is killing me.
I am alone in this world.
I'm going to have a heart attack.
That's the story of my life.
I hate that.
I'm slow.
People are rude.
I never get it right.
I don't have enough time.
I screw up all the time.
I have the worst luck.
I don't like my body.
I'm tired of this.
He insulted me.
I'm a mess.
I'm not any good.
I always forget.
He's a jerk.
I'm unattractive.
I'm fat.
I always lose at games.
I have a bad memory.
This always happens to me.

(NOTE: Take a deep breath and release all of these low-vibe thoughts from your mind, body and spirit.)

Appendix B

How to Use High-vibe Affirmations

1. High-vibe affirmations are high vibration statements, stated in the first person. i.e.: I am, I feel, I know. (While high-vibe thoughts are any thought with a high vibration: i.e.: This is a great day. You are beautiful.)

2. The purpose of the affirmation is to tell your mind what you are creating in your life.

3. When creating affirmations, make sure the affirmation sounds like YOU. It should come from your being. It shouldn't sound like it belongs to someone else. It's OK if it's not true for you yet.

4. When stating affirmations, it is important to create good feelings inside you. The affirmations work better when you feel good.

5. However, often times you are stating the affirmation because you don't feel good! Here is what to do:

6. Focus your attention on what lifts your energy and makes you feel good.

7. Then, state the affirmation repeatedly while focusing on good feelings. Remember, repetition is key.

Appendix C
Thinking Habits Exercises

EXERCISE: THINKING HABIT #1
I notice my thoughts.

My first thought when I wake in the morning:

_____

What I think about when I drink my coffee or tea:

_____

What I think about driving to school or work:

_____

What I think about when I am going to sleep:

_____

The top three topics I think about most. Are my thoughts high or low-vibe on these topics?

1. _____

Circle: My thoughts are mostly **high-vibe** or **low-vibe.**

2. _____

Circle: My thoughts are mostly **high-vibe** or **low-vibe.**

3. _____

Circle: My thoughts are mostly **high-vibe** or **low-vibe.**

EXERCISE: THINKING HABIT #2
I ask myself if what I'm thinking about is true.

Sometimes I assume that:

1.

2.

3.

Sometimes I worry about:

1.

2.

3.

More accurate thoughts:

1.

2.

3.

4.

5.

EXERCISE: THINKING HABIT #3
I choose good thoughts throughout the day.

Make a list of high-vibe thoughts (i.e.: Today is a
great day) and affirmations (i.e.: I am, I feel, I know,
etc.) that resonate with you, and make you feel good.

1.

2.

3.

4.

5.

6.

7.

8.

9.

10.

11.

12.

13.

14.

15.

10.

17.

18.

EXERCISE: THINKING HABIT #4
I feel my emotions without dwelling on them.

FACE:
Balancing Feeling and Thinking ™

1. FACE: I feel sad. My heart aches. I notice my stomach is like a knot.
2. ACCEPT: I accept that I feel sad. I do not judge myself for feeling. It's OK to be sad.
3. CHOOSE: I have compassion for myself. I've been here before. I'll get through this.
4. EXHALE: Breathe

1. I feel:

I accept how I feel:

I choose to think:

Breathe!

2. I feel:

I accept how I feel:

I choose to think:

Breathe!

3. I feel:

I accept how I feel:

I choose to think:

Breathe!

EXERCISE: THINKING HABIT #5
I regularly take a break from thinking.

Ways I take a break from thinking:

1.

2.

3.

Not thinking is hard for me because:

1.

2.

3.

Not thinking feels good to me because:

1.

2.

3.

EXERCISE: THINKING HABIT #6
I do not look for ways to be offended.

I've recently been offended by this person or situation:

_____

_____

I was hurt or angry because:

_____

_____

USE FACE: Balancing Feeling and Thinking

1. Face the feeling fully: I feel angry. I feel hurt.
   Notice where you feel it in your body.
2. Accept the feeling: It's OK that I'm angry.
3. Choose a good thought that lifts your energy.
i.e.: I will not take this personally. I will not give
away my power.
4. Exhale and breathe.

Other thoughts that could help you when you feel
you've been offended or insulted.

1.

2.

3.

EXERCISE: THINKING HABIT #7
I ask for help when I need it.

An area in my life where I have exhausted all my resources and I need help:

_____

_____

_____

What I've tried so far:

_____

_____

_____

I need help because:

_____

_____

_____

EXERCISE A: THINKING HABIT # 8
I think of what I'm grateful for
at the start of each day.

I am grateful for: (situations, people, places,
environments, talents, gifts, opportunities, etc.)

1.

2.

3.

4.

5.

6.

7.

8.

EXERCISE B: THINKING HABIT # 8

Make a list of what you enjoy doing. Even the small, seemingly insignificant activities, rituals, and things that make you smile, relax, or feel safe.

1.

2.

3.

4.

5.

6.

7.

8.

Appendix D
List of Figures

Recommended Reading

Power Vs. Force, The Hidden Determinants of Human Behavior, by David R. Hawkins, M.D., Ph.D. Hay House, Inc. 1995, 1998, 2002.

The True Power of Water, Healing and Discovering Ourselves, by Masaru Emoto. New York, Atria Books, 2003.

The Cosmic Code, Quantum Physics as the Language of Nature, by Heinz R. Pagels. Bantam Books, 1984.

As a Man Thinketh, by James Allen. DeVorss Publications. Original publication 1902.

The Power of Positive Thinking, by Norman Vincent Peale. Original publication 1952. Ballantine Books, 1996.

What to Say When You Talk to Yourself, by Shad Helmstetter, Ph.D. New York, Pocket Books, 1982.

The Biology of Belief, Unleashing the Power of Consciousness, Matter & Miracles, by Bruce Lipton, Ph.D. Santa Rosa, Elite Books, 2005.

Wherever You Go There You Are, Mindfulness Meditation in Everyday Life, by Jon Kabat-Zinn. New York, Hyperion, 2005.

Care of the Soul, A Guide for Cultivating Depth and Sacredness in Everyday Life, By Thomas Moore. New York, Harper Perennial, 1992.

The Brain That Changes Itself: Stories of Personal Triumph from the Frontiers of Brain Science, by Norman Doidge, MD. New York, Penguin Books, 2007.

www.8SimpleThinkingHabits.com

www.ingramcontent.com/pod-product-compliance
Lightning Source LLC
Chambersburg PA
CBHW021146090426
42740CB00008B/971

* 9 7 8 0 9 8 5 1 6 3 5 2 5 *